Birds

Teaching Tips

Green Level 5

This book focuses on the phonemes **/ea/ir/**.

Before Reading

- Discuss the title. Ask readers what they think the book will be about. Have them briefly explain why.
- Ask readers to sort the words on page 3. Read the sounds and words together.

Read the Book

- Encourage readers to break down unfamiliar words into units of sound. Then, ask them to string the sounds together to create the words.
- Urge readers to point out when the focused phonics phonemes appear in the text.

After Reading

- Encourage children to reread the book independently or with a friend.
- Ask readers to name other words with /ea/ or /ir/ phonemes. On a separate sheet of paper, have them write the words.

5357 Penn Avenue South
Minneapolis, MN 55419
www.jumplibrary.com

Decodables by Jump! are published by Jump! Library.

Library of Congress Cataloging-in-Publication Data is available at www.loc.gov or upon request from the publisher.

ISBN: 979-8-88524-748-1 (hardcover)
ISBN: 979-8-88524-749-8 (paperback)
ISBN: 979-8-88524-750-4 (ebook)

Photo Credits

Images are courtesy of Shutterstock.com. With thanks to Getty Images, Thinkstock Photo and iStockphoto.
Cover – Eric Isselee, Szczepan Klejbuk, Super Prin, Bachkova Natalia. 4&5 – Sacharewicz Patryk, AlekseyKarpenko. 6&7 – Sean Xu, Stefan Rotter, 8&9 – FJAH, Peter Turner Photography. 10&11 – WildMedia, Gallinagomedia. 12&13 – Ondrej Prosicky, 14&15 – AnnGaysorn, somdul. 16 – Shutterstock.

Can you sort the words on this page into two groups?

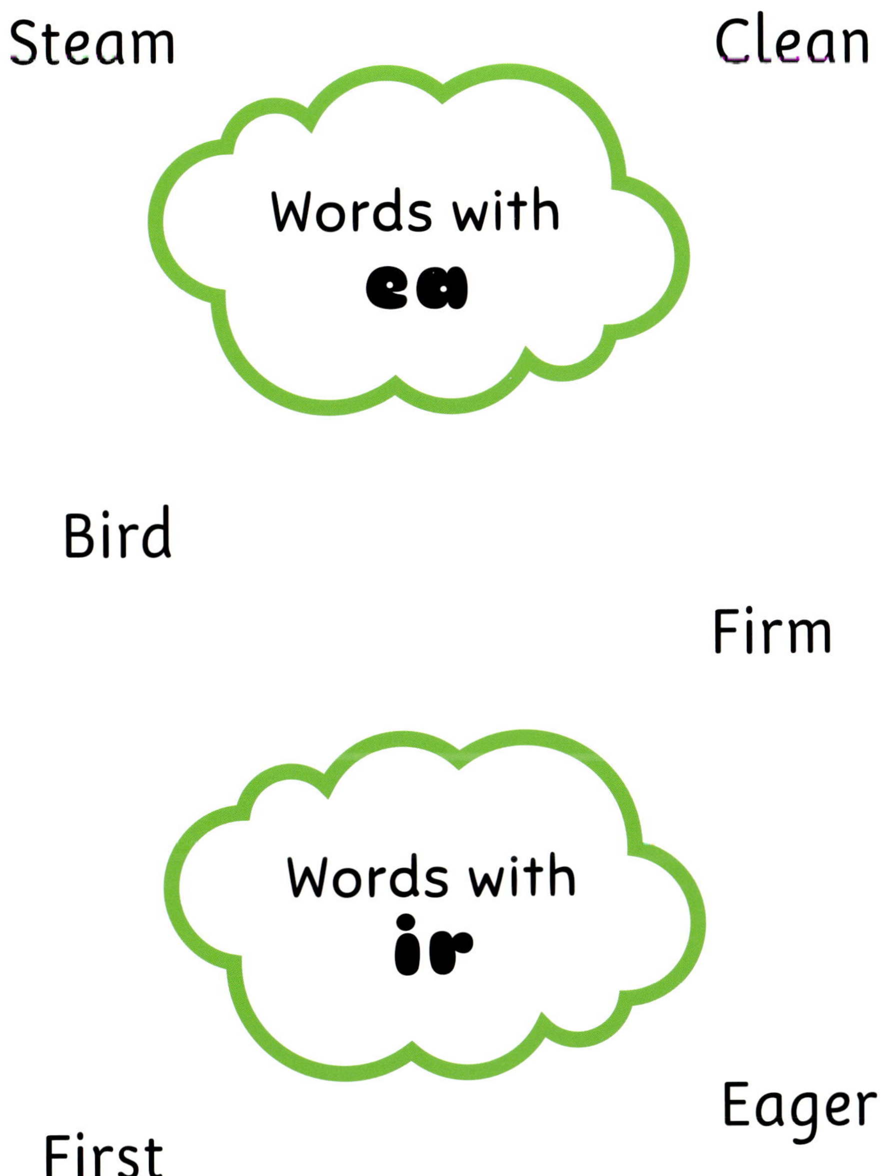

Have you seen a bird in the garden?
How about at the park?

A bird has a pair of wings, a pair of feet, and a strong beak.

You might spot a seagull at the beach.
Its beak has a little hook at the end.

Look out when you have food. Seagulls can steal food out of people's hands!

Have you seen a little brown bird with a big, red chest? This bird is called a robin.

Robins eat lots of things. They might look in the dirt to grab an insect.

Some birds like to sing songs. They can speak with the songs that they sing.

Songbirds can sing with lots of sounds.
Songbirds can chirp all day and night.

Owls are birds that you might see at night. You may see them in the woods.

You may hear an owl at night. It can go "twit twoo." Can you do that sound?

Grab paper and a pen. Sit in the garden or at the park and jot down the birds you see.

Jot down what sort of beaks they have and if they sing or chirp to you!

Sound out each word. Does it have an /ea/ or /ir/ sound?